Carolyn Slaughter

FOLLOWING
JESUS

steps to a
passionate faith

ABINGDON PRESS
NASHVILLE

FOLLOWING JESUS:
STEPS TO A PASSIONATE FAITH

Copyright © 2008 by Abingdon Press
All rights reserved.

This book is printed on acid-free paper.

ISBN 978-0-687-64958-7

08 09 10 11 12 13 14 15 16 17 – 10 9 8 7 6 5 4 3 2 1
MANUFACTURED IN THE UNITED STATES OF AMERICA

TABLE OF CONTENTS

INTRODUCTION

Welcome to *Following Jesus: Steps to a Passionate Faith*. Whether you are reading this book as part of a small-group study or exploring on your own, I hope that you find Scripture, ideas, prayers, and questions that guide you to a deeper understanding and fuller grasp of your relationship with God. In this study, you'll be searching for answers about the identity of Jesus and his role in your life, you'll discover more about your own spiritual gifts for ministry and new ways to be in service, and you'll think more deeply about what it means to be part of the church, the community of Christ.

Each time I lead a new group of Christians through this material, I learn something new about the Bible, about myself, about my relationship with God through Jesus Christ—and my passion for loving and serving God continues to grow. May God bless your journey as you explore the next steps in growing your own passionate faith.

Part 1
Rediscovering Jesus

1

SESSION ONE
JESUS THE MESSIAH

Who is Jesus?
A great teacher. A compelling
moral leader. An example of faith. A good man.
A visionary prophet. The Son of God.
Jesus is known by many names.

People have many opinions about who Jesus is, but many of those opinions are not based on an authoritative source. Unfortunately, many ideas about who Jesus is are opinions without much basis; we often simply adopt the ideas of those around us without our own thorough investigation. To know who Jesus really is we will go to the most authoritative source we know, one that will give us the facts about Jesus. We will base our investigation in the Bible.

Origin of the Bible

Read 2 Timothy 3:16-17
"All scripture is inspired by God and is useful for teaching, for reproof, for correction, and for training in righteousness, so that everyone who belongs to God may be proficient, equipped for every good work."

The Bible is a Christian's fact base—the basis of faith and life practices. As we learn in 2 Timothy 3:16, the Bible is God-breathed, the very words of God whispered into the hearts and ears of its human writers. It is God's tool used to transform and equip us to do God's work.

The word *bible* comes from the Greek *ta biblia*, meaning "the scrolls" or "the books." Although today we think of the Bible as a single work, it is actually a group of books written by a variety of authors. They were first written on individual scrolls of paper; but around 450 B.C. the documents were edited and compiled into what we now call the Old Testament.

Quick Bible Facts
66 books, written over a 1,600-year period, about 50 different human authors

Old Testament
39 books, from Creation to 50 B.C.

New Testament
27 books, from Jesus' birth to A.D. 100

The Bible, with all its books and contributors, tells one story from Genesis to Revelation: the story of a loving God who created human beings to be in relationship with God.

Following Jesus' death and resurrection, various witnesses (or disciples of eyewitnesses) recorded the life of Jesus and the early church. Included in these writings were also letters of instructions to new churches across the Middle East. Together, these writings are what we call the New Testament. The list of books to be included in the New Testament was finalized in A.D. 376 and is the New Testament we know today.

Prophesy of the Coming Messiah

The pursuit of who Jesus is actually takes a lifetime of discovery! In this session, we will focus on insights on Jesus from the Old Testament.

There are more than 300 references to the person called the Messiah in the Old Testament. *Messiah* was the Hebrew term for the person God would send to free God's people and bring them into personal relationship with God. The Greek term was *Christ* (meaning *Savior*). As we explore the Old Testament together, we will look at key prophecies that give specific insights about the coming Messiah—what this person would be like and what this person would do. Then we will look in the New Testament to see how those prophecies were fulfilled in Jesus.

In Isaiah 48:3-6, God told the world the purpose of the Old Testament prophecies:

Study Tip
Bible studies usually focus on portions of Scripture for explanations; however, you should always read the surrounding verses to help determine the meaning and ensure what the Bible really says.

I foretold the former things long ago, my mouth announced them and I made them known; then suddenly I acted, and they came to pass. For I knew how stubborn you were; the sinews of your neck were iron, your forehead was bronze. Therefore I told you these things long ago; before they happened I announced them to you so that you could not say, "My images brought them about; my wooden image and metal god ordained them." You have heard these things; look at them all. Will you not admit them? (NIV)

God knows how stubborn humans are and that how, left to our own devices, we will come up with our own reasons for whatever happens. But God wanted us to know who was in control of all that was being done. No credit was to go to false gods of wood and bronze, so we were given clues to God's work. God said to the world: *this is how you identify my plan. When all of these signs and prophecies come together, that is my person—the Messiah (savior of the world).*

The following verses are a representative sampling of prophecies. Each Old Testament prophecy is connected with its New Testament fulfillment. Examine each grouping for information about the Messiah and how this prophecy was fulfilled in Jesus, and then write down your insights on the lines that follow:

Isaiah 7:14; Matthew 1:18-25

_____
_____
_____
_____
_____
_____

Micah 5:2; Luke 2:1-7

_____
_____
_____
_____
_____
_____

Isaiah 40:3; Matthew 3:1-3 and 11:7-11

_____
_____
_____
_____
_____
_____

Isaiah 35:3-6; Matthew 9:27-35 and 11:1-6

_____
_____
_____
_____
_____

Zechariah 9:9; Luke 19:28-36

_____

_____

_____

_____

_____

_____

Isaiah 53:4-6, 11-12; Luke 23:32-34; 2 Corinthians 5:18-21

_____

_____

_____

_____

_____

_____

All of the prophecies came together in Jesus. As a result, persons all through the New Testament pointed to the fulfillment of prophecy to authenticate who Jesus is. Note here what people in the New Testament said about Jesus:

John 1:43-45 (*Philip, one of Jesus' disciples*)

_____

_____

_____

_____

Luke 24:44-48 (*Jesus himself*)

_____

_____

_____

_____

Acts 17:1-4 *(the apostle Paul, who had previously persecuted followers of Christ)*

_____

_____

_____

_____

Who Do You Say That I Am?

The question *Who is Jesus?* is one that everyone must answer at some point in his or her life. Jesus even asked his own disciples that very question while he was still in human form on earth. Read Matthew 16:13-16 to see how his disciples responded to this very important question:

> When Jesus came to the region of Caesarea Philippi, he asked his disciples, "Who do people say the Son of Man is?" They replied, "Some say John the Baptist; others say Elijah; and still others, Jeremiah or one of the prophets." "But what about you?" he asked. "Who do you say I am?" Simon Peter answered, "You are the Messiah, the Son of the living God."

Reflection

Based on what you know so far about Jesus, who do you say Jesus is? Write your response here:

_____

_____

_____

Prayer

Lord, I praise you for sending Jesus, the Messiah, to reconnect us with God forever and to serve as the ultimate example for the way we should live our lives. Thank you, God, for giving us your love story for humanity in written form. Please open my heart to a deeper walk with Jesus and empower me to live more fully for Jesus this week.

Homework

Spend time acquainting yourself with the Bible. Browse through the first four books of the New Testament—Matthew, Mark, Luke, and John. These are the books that primarily tell the story of Jesus. Read and complete Session Two.

2

SESSION TWO
THE UNIQUENESS OF JESUS

In the last session we learned from Scripture that hundreds of years before Jesus was born the prophets of Israel foretold the coming of Messiah—the Savior of the world. In this session we will explore more about the person of Jesus as we look at what Jesus' contemporaries said about him and what Jesus had to say about himself. Through our study, we will also discover some of the unique characteristics of Jesus. We are looking at all of this in the context of Matthew 16:15, "Who do you say that I am?"

What Makes Jesus Unique?

The following Scriptures reveal some of the unique qualities of Jesus. Read these Scriptures and ask who, what, when, where, and how questions for each verse. The answers to these questions will help you identify the context of the passage and give deeper meaning to what you are reading. Read not just to discover a single point but also to understand what the passage is saying to you.

Read each of the verses below and write down the unique characteristic about Jesus identified in that verse or group of verses.

• Matthew 1:18-25 _____
• John 8:28-30; 1 Peter 1:18-19; Luke 23:39-43 _____

_____

• Matthew 8:23-27; John 2:1-11 _____
• John 20:1-18; Matthew 9:23-26 _____
• Luke 7:40-50; Acts 10:39-43; Matthew 9:1-8 _____

_____

• John 6:28-35; 4:9-15 _____

He Said, They Said

What did Jesus say about himself?

In the Gospel of John, Jesus made many statements beginning with "I am" that helped his followers understand his identity and purpose. These include some memorable phrases like "I am the bread of life," "I am the light of the world," "I am the good shepherd," and "I am the way, the truth, and the life." Read the following Scriptures and write down what Jesus said about himself in each passage.

• John 4:21-26 _____

_____

• John 8:12 _____

_____

• John 10:7-15 _____

_____

• John 13:6-17 _____

_____

• John 14:5-10 _____

_____

• John 15:1-8 _____

_____

• John 17:1-5 _____

_____

What did Jesus' contemporaries say about him?

Many of the persons you will find in the following verses were the closest persons to Jesus when he was on earth. They lived and traveled with him in good times and bad. Jesus revealed his identity to them through teachings and stories, miracles and prayers. Some recognized Jesus for who he was immediately, while others grew into that understanding over time. Read the verses listed and write down what each person said about Jesus's identity and purpose.

• John 1:1-14 *(the disciple John)* _____

_____

• Matthew 16:16 *(the disciple Peter)* _____

_____

• John 11:27 *(Jesus' friend Martha)* _____

_____

• Acts 7:59 *(Stephen)* _____

_____

• John 20:26-29 *(the disciple Thomas)* _____

_____

• Colossians 1:15-20 *(Paul)* _____

_____

Christians believe there is strong evidence that Jesus is the Messiah, but how can we be confident that Jesus' contemporaries weren't fabricating stories about Jesus or lying about what they really knew or thought about him? Let's look at what two of Jesus' followers had to say about how the stories of Jesus were recorded for us.

Read Luke 1:1-4 and 1 John 1:1-3.

Summarize in your own words what these Scripture passages say about the authenticity of the biblical reports on Jesus:

_____

_____

_____

_____

Luke was a physician. We learn from his writings that Luke possessed a scientific mind and was interested in knowing and communicating the facts. He was not a person who let his imagination roam when writing about Jesus. Luke was a close friend and traveling companion of Paul. He was an eyewitness to the birth and growth of the early church and had access to the other disciples for information gathering. Luke took these eyewitness accounts and put them in organized form.

In the same way, John's Gospel and Letters are based on eyewitness accounts to the events of Jesus' life. In 1 John 1:1, John says "That which was from the beginning, which we have heard, which we have seen with our eyes, which we have looked at and our hands have touched—this we proclaim concerning the Word of life" (NIV).

These independent reports agree on who Jesus was and what he did.

Responding to Jesus

Because our goal in our Christian life is to be transformed, not merely informed, we must do something with the information we have been gathering. As we consider the question from Matthew 16, "Who do you say that I am?" we must begin narrowing the responses and make an individual, personal decision concerning Jesus. In John's Gospel, Jesus equates himself with God, and the testimonies of others agree. Now, each of us must choose to agree or disagree with them.

Reflection

Based on what you now know about Jesus, do you think he really is who he claims to be? Explain.

_____

_____

_____

What qualities or claims of Jesus do you find appealing?

_____

_____

_____

What qualities or claims of Jesus challenge you?

_____

_____

_____

If Jesus were physically in the room, would you like to meet him personally and spend time getting to know him? Why or why not?

_____

_____

_____

Prayer

I ask, God, for you to open my eyes and heart to your Word and the reality of who Jesus is. I pray that Jesus will become even more real to me and that he will reveal himself to me in even greater ways. Empower me this week to serve others and be all I can be for you.

Homework

Continue to explore the Gospels—the New Testament books of Matthew, Mark, Luke, and John—reading through some of the accounts of Jesus. Read and complete Session Three.

3

SESSION THREE
SAVIOR OF THE WORLD

Radical Transformation

The following excerpts are from the book *Spiritual Entrepreneurs* by Michael Slaughter (Abingdon Press, 1995). Read these quotations and then write your thoughts in response to the questions that follow.

I have visited many Sunday school classes when the people were...studying the lives of Abraham, Moses, David, or one of the other biblical characters. Information is given about 4,000-year-old people, and we feel that the purpose of the class has been accomplished. Scripture was not given for information. It was given that we might see the One who is the author of life and be radically transformed through him. (page 53)

Renewal happens as the church moves from a vague theism to a clear faith in Jesus Christ. The focus of the church is not church, but Jesus! God is made known to us in Christ. Faith comes alive in Christ. Lives are transformed and empowered through Christ. (page 32)

• What does it mean to be radically transformed?

_____

_____

_____

• How do you see transformation in lives of Christian people or through the church?

_____

_____

_____

• How do you see transformation happening in your own life?

_____

_____

_____

Why Did Jesus Come?

In today's session, we will focus on the source of life transformation: a personal relationship with Jesus. We will work through a short Bible study looking for the answers to the question, *Why did Jesus come?* This study is divided into three sections. Read through the Scriptures and reflect on the questions for each grouping to find out why Jesus came and what it means to follow him.

The Sin Problem

The Scriptures in this first section help us understand the human problem of sin, or separation from God. Read the following verses and answer the questions:

• What have we humans done to create our own problems?
○ Isaiah 53:6 _____
○ Romans 3:9-12 _____
○ Romans 3:23 _____
○ John 3:19 _____

• What are the consequences of our actions?
○ Isaiah 59:2 _____
○ Romans 6:23 _____
○ Romans 14:10-12 _____

How do you, in your own life, see actions or attitudes that separate you from God?

_____

_____

What one specific activity, fear, or habit do you see as the most critical in keeping you from becoming all God would hope for you?

_____

_____

We have all missed the mark in fulfilling God's design for us. There is no one exempt from the influence of our fallen nature. Likewise, there is no one exempt from the great love of God.

"We all, like sheep, have gone astray, we have all turned to our own way; and the LORD has laid on him the iniquity of us all." (Isaiah 53:6)

The Jesus Remedy

We've talked about our human condition of sin and the gulf that sin creates between us and the God who created us. Let's read now to understand how Jesus changes the equation. Again address the following questions through study of the Scriptures listed:

• How did Jesus' coming help us?

○ Isaiah 53:4-5 _____

○ Romans 5:8-9 _____

○ Titus 3:3-7 _____

○ Ephesians 2:8-9 _____

What does the word "grace" mean to you? How do you see it as a "gift" from God?

_____

_____

_____

Listen to the good news and the answer to our sin problem: Romans 5:8-9, "But God demonstrates his own love for us in this: While we were still sinners, Christ died for us. Since we have now been justified by his blood, how much more shall we be saved from God's wrath through him!" (NIV).

That's called grace—the totally undeserved, unearned, no-strings-attached, free gift of God.

Repentance and Forgiveness

We know that Jesus came to offer hope, salvation, and a way back to relationship with God. That way back comes through repenting or turning away from our sins, believing and welcoming Jesus into our lives and then fully experiencing forgiveness. Let's read more from Scripture on how that happens.

• What is our part in entering into a personal relationship with Christ and experiencing salvation? What steps must we take?

○ Isaiah 55:7 _____

○ 1 John 1:8-9 _____

○ Acts 16:31 _____

○ John 1:12 _____

What must we do to receive salvation in Jesus and enter into a personal relationship with him? The first step is to confess our sin and agree with God that we have been choosing to live life our way, not God's way. Next, we add to confession our repentance, which is a change in heart and a purposeful turning toward God. We turn around 180 degrees to be heading away from sin and to God. The next step is to believe. The New Testament word that we translate *believe* has the actual meaning "to lean your whole weight upon." In other words, this is an active word, so much more than just an intellectual concept. It is a lifestyle of movement toward and dependence on God. We receive Christ into our hearts by faith. Jesus comes into our lives just as a guest comes into our home when we open the door; only Jesus comes for a lifelong stay—sleeping bag and all! He only needs to be invited.

> "If we confess our sins, he who is faithful and just will forgive us our sins and cleanse us from all unrighteousness." (1 John 1:9, NRSV)

Now let's look at the next question, finding our answers from Scripture once again:

- What does salvation in Jesus mean to us?
○ Romans 4:23-5:2 _____
○ Romans 8:1-2 _____
○ 2 Corinthians 5:17 _____
○ John 5:24 _____

To be justified means to be made clean, or "just-as-if-I'd" never sinned. Salvation means I am at peace with God—all the guilt of past failures has been removed. Because Jesus paid the price for us we are removed from judgment, we move from eternal separation from God to an eternity living in God's presence. We have a new life and brand new start in life. The original Greek language used in the New

Testament includes a verb tense we don't have in English that gives rich meaning to God's intent for us. In the Greek, 2 Corinthians 5:17 says, "The old has gone and is continuing to go; the new has come and is continuing to come." We are in process in Jesus, being made new and whole every day as we practice repentance, confession, and depending on God. There is never a lack of fresh starts with Jesus.

> "Therefore, if anyone is in Christ, the new creation has come: The old has gone, the new is here!" (2 Corinthians 5:17)

What Does It Mean to Be a Christian?

It may take a lifetime to know how to live your Christian life; but what does it mean, in simple terms, to *be* a Christian? A Christian is someone who has repented of his or her sinful independence from God, surrendered control to Jesus, received the gift of eternal life, and made a faith commitment to follow Jesus for the rest of his or her life. A Christian's life is grounded in walking with Jesus daily. We are multi-dimensional people, and we respond to a relationship with Christ and our relationships with others on different levels. We use our intellect, our emotions, and our will. Being a Christian is the commitment of our whole being to Jesus Christ—all that we know of ourselves to all that we know of Jesus.

The Benefits of Following Jesus

Read each of the verses listed below and identify the benefit found in that passage.

- 2 Corinthians 5:17 _____
- John 3:16 _____
- Romans 8:9 _____
- Galatians 5:22-23 _____
- Philippians 4:19 _____

Knowing Jesus is an exciting thing! We are given a new start in life, initially when we ask Jesus into our lives, and every day as we turn our lives over to him and recommit to him once again. We are given eternal life, the promise of being in the presence of God through eternity. We are given the Holy Spirit who literally takes up residence in our lives and is the ongoing presence of Jesus within us. We are given Christ's trans-

> "For God so loved the world that he gave his only Son, so that everyone who believes in him may not perish but may have eternal life. Indeed, God did not send the Son into the world to condemn the world, but in order that the world might be saved through him."
> (John 3:16-17, NRSV)

forming power, which is the force creating radical transformation within us and will, over a lifetime, make us over into his image. We are given all the resources of God the Father to live this life of faith.

Reflection

If the news of salvation is a new message to you and you believe that the Bible's message about Jesus is true, maybe it is time for you to accept that message and make a faith commitment to Jesus. Talk to your study leader, your pastor, or another person of faith about your decision to follow Jesus.

Prayer

Thank you, Jesus, for what you did on the cross for me, for the restitution made on my behalf, and the price fully paid for my sin. I confess that I have been less than what you had in mind for me and have chosen to live life my own way and in my own efforts. Please forgive me and make me new. Thank you, Jesus, for the changes you will bring about in my life and for loving me so deeply.

Homework

Read and complete Session Four.

4

SESSION FOUR
LORD OF ALL

In this session, we're going to explore several areas related to authority in order to get us thinking about the implications of the profound fact that Jesus is Lord. Using Scripture as a guide, we will explore three areas: the differences between kingdoms and democracies, the differences between bondservants and volunteers, as well as who is in control of our resources. As we discuss each area, keep in mind that the ultimate goal is to answer the question, *What does it mean to make Jesus Lord of my life?*

Kingdom vs. Democracy

Here are some ideas on how kingdoms and democracies differ:

Democracy

- A democracy is headed by elected leaders who can be changed based on their popularity with people.
- A democracy allows participation by members of that democracy in the decision-making process. The people can change the rules.
- The leadership in a democracy represents the people.

Kingdom

- A king rules on the basis of his birth and is king for life.
- A kingdom is ruled by a king who gives decrees and expects obedience. Approval by the people is not involved.
- In a kingdom, the people represent the king.

List here any other differences you can identify:

_____

_____

_____

Would you say your household is more like a kingdom or a democracy? What about your workplace?

_____

_____

_____

Look up the following verses, noting what each passage says in the space provided. Then use that information to answer the questions that follow.

- Luke 23:1-3 _____
- Matthew 6:9-10 _____

- 1 Timothy 6:13-16 _____
- Revelation 19:11-16 _____

From these verses, is Christianity more like a democracy or a king-dom?

_____
_____
_____

What does that mean for followers of Jesus?

_____
_____
_____

In what practical ways should life be different because of the absolute authority of Jesus?

_____
_____
_____

Jesus came as King of kings and Lord of lords, ruler over all. Being in relationship with Jesus means becoming part of his kingdom and submitting to his rule and authority. This requires obedience to his commands on our part.

Servant or Volunteer

The thought of being a servant is not normally a pleasing one to us, yet the term Jesus chose to use to describe his followers was *slave* or *servant*. Servanthood represents a loss of control over our lives. We like to say, "I volunteer my time at the church," meaning we feel good about donating some of our time; but we still like to be able to decide our limits, set our boundaries, protect ourselves, and to pick and choose what we will or will not do based on what is convenient for us.

Read Matthew 20:25-28 and paraphrase it here:

_____

_____

_____

The original disciples saw themselves as anything but volunteers. As part of a society based on the institution of slavery, they clearly understood a slave's role and a slave's relationship to his or her master.

Read the following verses and write down the terms Jesus' followers used in introducing themselves:

• Philippians 1:1 _____

• James 1:1 _____

• Revelation 1:1 _____

• Titus 1:1 _____

While volunteers are concerned with themselves, their convenience, and their ability to choose and control, a servant has no agenda but that of his or her master. Giving ourselves over to the control of a master requires a deep level of trust.

Coming to Jesus is not just a continuation of life as it has been with the addition of God's blessing; rather, it is a life of obedience—submitting to Jesus' authority and doing what Jesus tells us to do. Obedience is more than lip service. It is a way of life in which we are no longer self-ruling individuals. God rules everything in our lives.

Who Is in Control?

Using the spaces provided, write down in the first column the five most valuable resources you possess. These may be material or financial possessions but could also include less tangible items such as time, talents, career, family, and other relationships. Next to each item, write in the second column the name of the person or institution that presently has authority and control over that resource. For example, if the resource is your house, the institution in authority over it may be the bank. If a person is listed as a valuable resource, that person probably is the authority over himself or herself. If time or talent is listed, the authority may be you.

1. _____   _____   _____
2. _____   _____   _____
3. _____   _____   _____
4. _____   _____   _____
5. _____   _____   _____

Read Acts 2:42-47 and 4:32-35.

• What do these verses say about the way the early disciples viewed their personal resources?

_____

_____

_____

• Who do you think was in control of the disciples' resources?

_____

_____

_____

• What were the results of this community putting their resources under Jesus' control?

_____

_____

_____

For each item you wrote down in the exercise at the top of the page, cross out the name of the person or institution that you listed in the second column as being in control of that resource; and write "Jesus Christ" in its place in the third column. Then, in the lines below, write a description of how your life might be different if you gave Jesus total control of each of the resources you listed.

_____

_____

_____

Read Matthew 7:21-27.

• Why do you think Jesus wants to be Lord of your life?

_____

_____

_____

• How would relinquishing control of your life to God benefit you?

_____

_____

_____

• What's the main thing that hinders you from letting Jesus be Lord of your life?

_____

_____

_____

To make Jesus "Lord" means to give him control over everything in our lives—all that we do, all that we own, all that we are. We live in an affluent society with an individualistic mentality, so giving up control is a major issue. We may feel uncomfortable or even fearful in handing Jesus control of our lives, but let's remember to whom we are giving control.

Trusting Jesus as Lord

Read Matthew 11:28-30.

• What will you find when you give Jesus control?

_____

_____

_____

This passage tells us of a master who wants to ease our load, not make our load heavier. Rather than removing us from productive work, Jesus offers his love and healing peace as we continue to serve him. Our trust in Jesus grows as we come to know him and understand his character and his loving intentions toward us.

Reflection

As we welcome Jesus into our lives and into our hearts, we enter into a relationship with him. We accept and relate to him as both Savior and Lord. If Jesus is Lord, then he has absolute authority over all areas of our lives. Think of the different areas of your life—your family, work, friends, health, finances, job, time, even hobbies. We cannot compartmentalize our lives, giving him authority over only one or two areas and keep the rest for ourselves. What would it look like if you truly gave God authority over your life through Jesus Christ?

Take these next moments to be silent and allow Jesus to show you where you need to let him be Lord. As he shows you each area of your life that you need to let him control, surrender that area to him; and then pray for him to have complete authority in your life.

Prayer

Lord Jesus, I thank you for being in control of all things—including my life. I offer you the areas of my life that I have not surrendered

37

to you; transform them to honor you. Strengthen me in living under your Lordship. Thank you for your care for me

Homework

Read the information on baptism below and bring any questions you have to your study leader. Read and complete Session Five.

What Is Baptism?

Baptism, in some form, is a requirement for membership for many denominations. Baptism is a public statement of your entry into a personal relationship with Jesus Christ. It is the outward *sign* of your salvation, not its *source*. There are at least three ways of addressing baptism. Ask your study leader or pastor about baptism at your church.

Elements of Baptism

1. Recognition of baptism as an infant or young child is an acknowledgment of the faith statement made by parents or guardians on a child's behalf. It affirms that God is involved and active in the child's life. An adult who was baptized as an infant or child is not required to be baptized again.
2. Baptism of a new believer as a sign of your new relationship with Jesus Christ. This is done in two ways:
   a. Sprinkling. This method involves having water dripped over your head by a pastor during a baptism service.
   b. Immersion. This method involves being totally submerged under water. A pastor does this during a baptism service.
3. Reaffirmation of baptism. This applies to persons who have already been baptized, but desire to make a public statement of faith concerning their deeper relationship or renewed commitment with Christ. A pastor places the sign of the cross on the person's forehead.

Part 2
Growing in the Spirit

5

SESSION FIVE
THE HOLY SPIRIT

Most of us understand who God the Father is, who Jesus is, and the relationship between the Father and the Son. However, when we add the Holy Spirit to the conversation, we sometimes become confused.

Scripturally, the Trinity is explained as three distinct persons in relationship with one another who exist as one Godhead—a true mystery. It's helpful to use models to help us understand how God can be Father, Son, and Holy Spirit—and yet remain one God. One model that illustrates the Trinity is water in three forms—liquid, ice, and steam. Each form coexists with the others but at the same time is separate and distinct from the others. All three forms have the same chemical equation—H_2O—as their base, which remains constant no matter what form the water takes. Another model is an egg, which is made up of three distinct parts: the yolk, the white, and the shell. Each part looks different and has a distinct purpose, but at the most basic level all three have the DNA of egg. The coexisting three persons of God are separate and distinct from each other, yet have the same nature and attributes. At the core, all three are equally God.

The Trinity is mysterious and not easy to understand, but is critical to our faith. It has been said, "The person who tries to understand the Trinity will surely lose his mind...but the person who denies the Trinity will surely lose his soul."

In this session, our goal is to answer two questions: *Who is the Holy Spirit?* and *What is the Spirit's role in our lives?*

The Holy Spirit Personality Profile

The Scriptures listed below will give you insight into the Holy Spirit. Look up the verses and write what you find out about the Spirit. In the first exercise, we are looking for characteristics of a personality or personhood. These characteristics remind us that we are relating to the Holy Spirit as a person rather than an undefined, formless entity.

* Romans 8:27 _____
* 1 Corinthians 2:9-13 _____
* 1 Corinthians 12:11 _____
* Romans 15:30; Ephesians 4:30; Hebrews 10:29 _____

"Therefore go and make disciples of all nations, baptizing them in the name of the Father and of the Son and of the Holy Spirit." (Matthew 28:19)

Matthew 28:19-20 reminds us that the Holy Spirit is God, equal with the Father and the Son. The Spirit has all the attributes, power, and wisdom that God possesses. In Scripture, the Holy Spirit is called the Spirit of God and the

Spirit of Christ, as well as the Holy Spirit. And if you are a follower of Jesus, the Holy Spirit lives within your spirit. It is essential to grasp the fact that the Spirit has the characteristics of a person—such as an intellect, a means of communication, emotions, and a will—so that we can understand the reality of our continual personal relationship with God through the Spirit. As we experience the Spirit's personality, we see God and get to know God on a personal level. The Holy Spirit enables believers to know and walk with God by being present, active, and responsive in our lives every day.

Holy Spirit Movements

As one-third of the Trinity, the Holy Spirit has always been active in God's plan for the world. The Holy Spirit is mentioned all through the Old Testament, from Creation in Genesis 1 through the inspiration of the prophets at the end of the Old Testament. In the Old Testament, the Spirit was available to a few key individuals. For example, we read about the Spirit "coming upon" such people as David and Samson, giving them wisdom and power to do what God had called them to do. However, not everyone had or experienced the Spirit; and, as with King Saul, the Spirit did not always remain long-term with a person.

In the New Testament we can see that Jesus relied on the power of the Spirit during his time on earth. Philippians 2:5-8 tells us that Jesus set aside his power as God when he took on human form:

> Have the same attitude of mind Christ Jesus had: Who, being in very nature God, did not consider equality with God something to be used to his own advantage; rather, he made himself nothing by taking the very nature of a servant, being made in human likeness. And being found in appearance as a human being, he humbled himself by becoming obedient to death—even death on a cross!

The New Testament makes frequent references to Jesus being "full of the Spirit" as he fulfilled his ministry. Jesus lived his life on earth just as we have to live; he showed us how to depend on the Spirit moment by moment.

There is a distinct difference in how the Spirit acted between the Old Testament and the New Testament. In the New Testament, after Jesus' resurrection and ascension, the Spirit became available to everyone who is in a personal relationship with Jesus. Now, all followers of Jesus have the same power that was available to the greats of the Old Testament. However, instead of the Spirit "coming upon" people, now the Spirit lives within people. The Holy Spirit is present and active in our lives to empower us, but it's our choice as to how much we will allow the Spirit to do that.

The Role of the Holy Spirit

Listed below are Scriptures that describe the role of the Holy Spirit in our lives and in the world. Read each passage and write down how the Spirit works and what the Spirit accomplishes in and through us.

- John 14:25-26 _____
- John 15:26 _____
- John 16:7-11 _____
- John 16:12-15 _____
- Acts 1:8 _____
- Romans 8:14-17 _____
- 1 Corinthians 6:19-20 _____
- 1 Corinthians 12:7-11 _____
- Galatians 5:16-23 _____

Are there times when you have felt the Holy Spirit with you, guiding you?

_____

_____

What other roles have you felt the Holy Spirit play in your life?

_____

_____

Filled With the Spirit

There is a difference between "having" the Holy Spirit and being "filled with" the Spirit. Read the following Scriptures and record what they say.

• Acts 2:38 _____

• Romans 8:9 _____

The definition of a follower of Jesus is one who has the Spirit of God living in him or her, and this happens at the moment we open our lives to Jesus. So, all followers of Jesus have the Holy Spirit living within them. However, the filling of the Spirit is accomplished only when we choose to give up control over our own lives and allow the Holy Spirit to control and empower us.

Let's look at some examples of Spirit-filled Christians from Scripture. Read the following verses and describe what happened when ordinary people gave the Spirit control of their lives.

• Acts 4:8-13 _____

• Acts 4:31-35 _____

• Galatians 5:16-26 _____

We see dramatic effects on everyday people and entire communities. God uses people regardless of their background, even without formal education or training. And the Spirit addresses the inner tug of war going on between our human nature, which defaults to sin, and the Holy Spirit, who always takes God's way. Allowing the Spirit to control and empower us is our part in the transformation process.

45

The internal battle is real, and we will find ourselves dealing with choices all day long. Sometimes our choices do not please God. But as we surrender to the power of the Spirit, God makes changes in us, big and small, every day, until we are formed in the image of Christ. God uses our choices to teach and form us.

Reflection

Being filled with the Holy Spirit establishes Jesus as Lord of our lives. In what area of your life do you feel the Spirit moving? In what area do you need to let the Spirit more fully control and empower you?

Prayer

Thank you, God, for being such a personal God and choosing to live within me. Thank you for your goodness in supplying through the Holy Spirit all the resources I need to live life as you intend. I confess that I have taken control of my life and strayed from what you have desired for me. Now I breathe in the fullness of your love and forgiveness. Holy Spirit, fill me and make me new once again.

Homework

Read through and complete Session Six. Also complete the "Spiritual Fruit Inventory" activity (pp. 47–51).

Spiritual Fruit Inventory: Evaluating Your Spiritual Fruit

Most of us know how to evaluate fruit to tell whether it is good or bad to eat. There is also a way to evaluate how well we express the fruit of the Spirit in our lives. You can gauge your effectiveness in allowing the fruit of the Spirit to be demonstrated in your life by answering the following questions. When you are finished, tally your score to see which character qualities appear to be most evident in your life.

Based on your personal experience, respond to the following statements. Use the number system below to rank each statement.

0 = Never true for me   2 = True most of the time
1 = True every once in a while   3 = Definitely true for me

____ 1. I am grateful that God loved the world (and me!) so much that God's Son was sacrificed as our means of salvation.

____ 2. God's presence makes me glad.

____ 3. I rest in the fact that God is in control of all things—past, present, and future.

____ 4. Even though I don't always understand what's happening, I am willing to wait on God to act on my behalf.

____ 5. I am amazed by God's intense care for me shown by sending Jesus to take the punishment I deserve.

____ 6. I know that there are times when God is justified in being angry.

____ 7. I love the fact that Jesus set aside his power as God in order to reach out to broken and hurting people.

____ 8. I know that God will do exactly what God promises.

____ 9. My lifestyle reflects my obedience to God.

____10. I'm confident in God's love for me, even when I act in an unloving way toward others.

___11. I have an inner assurance of my relationship with Jesus.

___12. Because I have Jesus, I am calmer, even when problems come along.

___13. I accept others right where they are.

___14. I choose to forgive others because Jesus chooses to forgive me.

___15. I am immediately sensitive to the conviction of God's Spirit when I've done something wrong.

___16. When someone approaches me in anger, I generally don't react with the same harshness.

___17. People who know me well would say that I have a consistent walk with God.

___18. I say no to things that might hinder my communion with God.

___19. I am committed to serving others, even when I don't feel like it.

___20. Even when things go wrong, I have an inner assurance of God's presence.

___21. I am confident that my sins are forgiven.

___22. I don't complain about my problems; instead, I trust God.

___23. I comfort, encourage, and affirm others.

___24. I live a lifestyle that pleases God.

___25. Even when I feel attacked, I am committed to obeying God's Word and submitting to the Holy Spirit.

___26. I follow through with what I say I will do.

___27. I am committed to a consistent time alone with God for prayer and Bible study.

___28. I choose to be positive and affirm the good qualities of people, even when they get on my nerves.

___29. I have consistent satisfaction from doing what God wants me to do.

___30. I am confident that God accepts me because of my relationship with Jesus.

____31. I am content that God has me in process and will develop me into what God wants me to be.

____32. I speak positively to others to build them up.

____33. I am truthful, honest, and keep the promises I make.

____34. I seek to be humble, cooperative, and teachable all the time.

____35. I am responsible.

____36. I have asked my friends or a support group to hold me accountable for areas in which I struggle.

____37. I serve others with no expectations of being served in return.

____38. I have a deep sense of pleasure because I sense God's presence as I serve.

____39. I am not easily stressed out because I know God is in control.

____40. I am willing to wait for things that will benefit me physically, spiritually, or materially.

____41. I listen and try to understand others.

____42. I have confronted other Christians in a caring way when they have made wrong choices in the way they live.

____43. I am open and receptive to feedback in areas in which I need improvement.

____44. I use the abilities God has given me for God's glory.

____45. When I recognize a behavior problem in my life, I immediately act to bring it under control.

____46. When I have been hurt, I am willing to forgive and begin again with that person.

____47. I delight in what God is doing in the lives of others.

____48. I have a calm assurance even in difficult situations.

____49. When I am hurting, I place my hope in God.

____50. I am compassionate and respond to the needs of others.

____51. I am involved in serving others in my community and around the world in order to influence others for Jesus.

____52. Regardless of my feelings, I focus on doing what is right.

____53. Because I belong to God, I understand that my time, money, and energy are God's to use as God wishes.

___54. Distractions do not keep me from my goals.

___55. I pray for my enemies and for those who are difficult to love.

___56. No matter what I am doing, I am content because God is with me and is using me to serve others.

___57. I experience the Holy Spirit's comfort in the midst of the world's chaos.

___58. I accept others who are different from me.

___59. I treat others with kindness and generosity, even when they are different from me or rejected by others.

___60. I take a stand for truth and against injustice.

___61. I don't seek revenge when others hurt me.

___62. My friends know they can count on me.

___63. I stay away from situations in which I am easily tempted.

After completing the Inventory, place your answer beside each corresponding question number in the table on the next page.

Place your answer beside each corresponding question number in the table. Add the total in each horizontal row for your final score. There is a total possible score of 21 for each aspect of the fruit of the Spirit. The higher your score for each quality, the more likely you are to be demonstrating that quality in your life.

							Total	**Fruit**
1___	10___	19___	28___	37___	46___	55___	A___	Love
2___	11___	20___	29___	38___	47___	56___	B___	Joy
3___	12___	21___	30___	39___	48___	57___	C___	Peace
4___	13___	22___	31___	40___	49___	58___	D___	Patience
5___	14___	23___	32___	41___	50___	59___	E___	Kindness
6___	15___	24___	33___	42___	51___	60___	F___	Goodness
7___	16___	25___	34___	43___	52___	61___	G___	Gentleness
8___	17___	26___	35___	44___	53___	62___	H___	Faithfulness
9___	18___	27___	36___	45___	54___	63___	I___	Self-Control

6

SESSION SIX
FRUIT OF THE SPIRIT

One of the key concepts we touched on in the last session was how the Holy Spirit moves in our lives. One of the results of the Spirit's movement in our lives is what the Bible calls spiritual "fruit." Now let's explore that idea more in depth and discover what it means to bear spiritual fruit.

Fruit of the Spirit

In a Christian's life, there is an expectation that as we grow in our life of faith, we will begin to produce "fruit," or demonstrate results of living in Christ. As we give control over to the Holy Spirit living within us, the same results will be produced in our lives that Jesus demonstrated through his life. We will see two different things happen:

1. We will produce fruit by impacting people in such a way that they will be drawn to Jesus and their own personal relationship with him.

2. The fruit of the Spirit listed in Galatians 5:22-23 will be developed in our lives, resulting in the character of Christ shining through us. Our lives will reflect Jesus to those around us.

> "This is to my Father's glory, that you bear much fruit, showing yourselves to be my disciples." (John 15:8)
>
> "No good tree bears bad fruit, nor does a bad tree bear good fruit. Each tree is recognized by its own fruit. People do not pick figs from thornbushes, or grapes from briers. Good people bring good things out of the good stored up in their heart, and evil people bring evil things out of the evil stored up in their heart. For out of the overflow of the heart the mouth speaks." (Luke 6:43-45)

These two kinds of fruit are inter-related. People are attracted to a Christ-like lifestyle. People around us may even say to us, "You're different. I want what you have."

Lifestyle is an important issue in Christianity because of the far-reaching impact our lives have on others. Gandhi, known as the George Washington of India, was a Hindu—yet he was very familiar with Christianity. He has been quoted as saying he was extremely attracted to the person of Jesus. But he never converted to Christianity because of Christians, who he experienced to be so unlike their Christ. Obviously, the fruit of the Spirit in our lives impacts our ability to influence others for Jesus.

Read the following verses and name some of the key points about fruit from each passage.

• John 15:1-8 _____

_____

• Luke 6:43-45 _____

_____

• Galatians 5:22-23 _____

_____

The fruit of the Spirit you read about in Galatians 5:22-23 is not something we receive. Rather, it is a cluster of character qualities that are progressively produced in us through a life constantly yielded to the Holy Spirit. It is the work of the Holy Spirit in us, not something we produce ourselves. Our responsibility is to stay connected to our source of life and make conscious choices to yield and obey. As we grow and mature, over time we take on the qualities of our heavenly parent in increasingly more visible ways.

> "By contrast, the fruit of the Spirit is love, joy, peace, patience, kindness, generosity, faithfulness, gentleness, and self-control." (Galatians 5:22-23a, NRSV)

What Is the Fruit of the Spirit?

The fruit of the Spirit is not the same as the gifts of the Spirit. We will discuss in detail the gifts of the Spirit in Session Seven. What we need to know right now is that spiritual gifts are special empowerments for ministry. They are given to equip and build up the body of Christ. The gifts are what we do. The fruit of the Spirit is a grouping of character qualities visible in the life of each follower of Jesus. The fruit is who we are. No follower of Jesus is given all the spiritual gifts, but all of the nine character qualities listed in Galatians are to be evident in every follower's life.

Nine fruit of the Spirit (character qualities) are identified in Galatians 5:22-23. In each of the Scripture groupings on the next page, identify which of the nine fruit is described.

Characteristic 1:
Luke 6:32-36; John 3:16-17;
John 13:34-35; 1 John 4:19-21

Characteristic 2:
John 15:9-11; Acts 13:49-52;
Romans 14:17-18; Romans 15:13

Characteristic 3:
Isaiah 32:14-20; John 16:29-33;
Philippians 4:4-7; Romans 5:1-2

Characteristic 4:
Colossians 3:12-13; 2 Timothy 4:1-5;
Ephesians 4:1-2; 1 Thessalonians 5:14-15

Characteristic 5:
Romans 2:1-4; Ephesians 2:4-7;
Romans 11:22-23; Ephesians 4:32

Characteristic 6:
Romans 15:14-16; Ephesians 5:8-11;
2 Peter 1:3-4; Titus 2:11-15

Characteristic 7:
1 Corinthians 4:1-2; 3 John 2-5;
Matthew 25:14-23; Lamentations 3:22-24

Characteristic 8:
Matthew 11:28-30; Titus 3:1-2;
1 Corinthians 4:18-21; 1 Peter 3:13-16

Characteristic 9:
2 Timothy 3:1-5; 1 Timothy 1:7;
Titus 1:7-9; 1 Peter 5:8-11

Defining the Fruit of the Spirit

Love: the ability to unconditionally accept and love others based in this same quality offered to us by God through Jesus Christ; the ability to give ourselves in service to others without expecting anything in return. Love in the New Testament sense is not necessarily a feeling or emotion; it is doing the right thing toward another, even when you don't feel like it.

- *When have you seen this kind of love demonstrated?* _____

_____

Joy: a deep, inner gladness that results from an intimate relationship with Christ. It is maintained through obedience and is renewed through service to others. Joy is not dependent on circumstances but is a result of our communion with God. Joy is not just happiness or feeling good; those emotions depend on our circumstances and what is going on around us. Joy is what is produced within us as a result of living in obedience to Christ and prioritizing and serving others. Jesus demonstrated that we can have joy regardless of our circumstances—including suffering. Joy is produced in us as we focus on God and the end result God is bringing about in our lives, not on what we are experiencing.

- *Share a time when you experienced joy even when you weren't happy:* _____

_____

Peace: an inner harmony and sense of well-being based on our confident faith that God has accepted us, loves us, and is in control of our lives no matter how turbulent our external situation might be. Peace results from knowing we are forgiven and accepted by God. Peace does not require the absence of conflict or distress; it is a sense of tranquility and order regardless of what is happening around us because no matter our circumstances, God has everything in place and is in control.

• *Describe a time when you experienced God's peace:* _____

_____

Patience: the ability to exercise restraint and calmly persevere in waiting on God, despite people or circumstances that might provoke us or cause agitation. Patience is the ability to walk through life long-term, realizing God has a timetable for each process in our lives. Patience accepts consequences, endures the wrong of others, bears injuries and suffering for God, and refuses to retaliate. Being patient does not mean we are to deny our feelings, nor does it mean we cannot set boundaries with others. It does mean we have persistence and staying power.

• *Where in your life do you need patience?* _____

_____

Kindness: the ability to treat others with openness, sensitivity, and love—especially those who have specific needs we can meet. This ability is based on the kindness shown to us by God. Kindness deals not with our abilities but our attitudes. We can be extremely gifted in skills; yet our style, tone, and volume of voice can be hurtful. Kindness is the Christ-like way we treat others, and includes attitudes like compassion, mercy, friendliness, and loyalty.

• *Describe a time when you experienced the undeserved kindness of another:* _____

_____

Goodness: to have the nature of God, and therefore, to be able to discern right from wrong, do good to others, and expose evil and injustice. Goodness results from the Spirit developing within us the same sense of right and wrong God has. Loving confrontation comes from this character quality. Goodness may be expressed as taking a stand against wrong in the lives of others or in society. Goodness must always work hand-in-hand with kindness.

• *What example can you give of goodness in action?* _____

_____

Faithfulness: an unshakable loyalty displayed by being trustworthy, reliable, and responsible: completely carrying out commitments to God and others. Faithfulness means following through and fulfilling promises we make. Our commitment level is determined by this character quality. God is a God of covenant, or unbreakable promises, and is willing to stick with us regardless of our behavior or circumstances. God promises to never walk away from us, as Hebrews 13:5 assures us. Because this covenantal God lives within us, we are empowered to be faithful, too, in all our relationships and commitments.

• *How have you seen the faithfulness of God through others?* _____

_____

Gentleness: demonstrating consideration and thoughtfulness—putting my rights and strength willingly under God's control in order to handle myself in a calm manner. Gentleness requires openness, humility, and a teachable spirit, rather than the harshness originating from personal pride and selfishness. A gentle person is not a weak person; rather, this person has put his or her strength under the control of God. Like a tamed horse, that strength is now useful and focused.

• *Who in your life consistently demonstrates gentleness?* _____

_____

Self-control: to take responsibility for myself and exercise discipline in order to avoid sin and live a life that pleases God. Self-control is a choice to give God control over our lives. This results in a lifestyle that is appealing to God, and brings us the support and power of the Holy Spirit to prevent or overcome excesses.

• *Where do you need increased self-control?* _____

_____

Reflection

Using the results of your "Spiritual Fruit Inventory" (your homework from last week):

What three aspects of spiritual fruit are most evident in your life?

_____

_____

_____

Where have you seen these in operation in your life?

_____

_____

_____

Developing Your Fruit

The wonderful truth about the Christian life is we are all on a progressive journey. Each of us demonstrates the fruit of the Spirit differently and will grow at different rates. It is similar to the development of an apple. In the spring, blossoms form on the apple trees and are soon pollinated. The blossoms fade and dry up, and are replaced with the bud of an apple. Over weeks and months the bud develops into a little green apple, which grows in size and color. By fall, the apple is red and lusciously sweet, ready to be picked. The apple is exactly what God had in mind. Each of us is in one of the developmental stages of the apple. Some of us are just budding, others are little green apples, and some are developing the color and sweetness of mature fruit. Every stage of development is essential and is necessary for the next stage to happen. Even if we are little hard, sour apples right now, we are right where God wants and needs us to be. We can't grow bigger and better without being where we are now. It is important for the little green apple to stay attached to its parent plant so it can come to full growth. Likewise, it is important for us to stay attached to Jesus for us to ripen and mature into the people God has in mind, demonstrating the fruit of God's presence in our lives.

Prayer

Thank you, God, for being my source of life and growth, the vine to which I seek to stay attached. I am so thankful for your investment in my transformation process. May your character qualities increasingly grow in me, and may those around me increasingly see Jesus through me.

Homework

Complete a spiritual gifts assessment using the Internet or other resources as directed by your study leader. Also read and complete Session Seven.

7

SESSION SEVEN
GIFTS OF THE SPIRIT

Using the hand you normally write with, write your name here:

Now change to your other hand, and write your name here:

How does it feel to do something that was not natural to you?

_____

_____

How do you feel about the results? _____

_____

Many people within the church have this same uncomfortable feeling when they try to serve in a way that is not natural to them. And the results can be disastrous!

God has prepared each of us to serve within the church. Part of this preparation is giving you one or more spiritual gifts. Not all of us are gifted in the same way. God has not used a cookie cutter to stamp out people in a process of uniformity. That's why it feels awkward for you to serve the body of Christ in a way that does not suit how God has designed you and gifted you.

What is a spiritual gift anyway? A spiritual gift is a supernatural power within you to serve others. It is more than a human talent or a skill that you have learned; it is the work of the Holy Spirit in your life, empowering you in a specific way to serve well. It is how the Spirit chooses to be revealed through you . . . as a teacher, a helper, an administrator, or any of the other spiritual gifts.

Defining Spiritual Gifts

There are three primary passages in the Bible that list the spiritual gifts. Read the following Scripture passages, and list the spiritual gifts named in each:

Romans 12:4-8; 1 Corinthians 12:4-11, 27-31; Ephesians 4:11-13

What does 1 Corinthians 12:12-26 say about the importance of each gift?

_____

_____

_____

Some of the gifts are listed once, but others are listed in more than one of these passages. All together there are twenty different gifts mentioned within the three Scripture references. Let's explore these twenty in more detail.

Read through the definition for each of the spiritual gifts and, using the space provided, identify one way in which you may see that gift operating within the church.

GROUP 1

Exhortation (encouragement)—the ability to encourage people and assist them in moving toward spiritual maturity and personal wholeness. This gift uses the skills of comfort and confrontation, encouragement and instruction. _____

Giving—the ability to give of material wealth freely and with joy to further God's causes. Use of this gift provides physical resources in response to assessed needs. _____

Leadership—the ability to see "the big picture" and assemble the component parts through the ability to motivate, coordinate, and direct the efforts of others in doing God's work. _____

_____

GROUP 2

Teaching—the ability to understand and clearly communicate God's truths to others in ways that lead them to apply God's truth to their lives. _____

Prophecy—the ability to proclaim God's truth in a way that's relevant to current situations and to envision how God would will things to change. _____

65

Mercy—the ability to perceive the suffering of others and to minister to them effectively with empathy and without condemnation. _____

GROUP 3
Serving—demonstrating God's love through the ability to identify the needs of others and selflessly working to meet them. _____

Wisdom—the ability to understand and apply biblical and spiritual knowledge to practical, everyday problems. _____

Knowledge—the ability to understand, organize, and effectively use information, from either natural sources or the Holy Spirit directly, for the advancement of God's purposes. _____

GROUP 4
Faith—the ability to recognize what God wants to accomplish and the steadfast confidence that God will see it done despite what others perceive as barriers. _____

Healing—the ability to effectively call on God for the curing of illness and the restoration of health in a supernatural way. _____

Discernment of spirits—the ability to recognize what is of God and what is not of God. _____

Helps—the ability to work alongside others and see the value of accomplishing practical and often behind-the-scenes tasks that promote God's kingdom. _____

GROUP 5
Speaking in tongues—the ability to supernaturally speak in a language, known or unknown to others, with no prior knowledge of that language. _____

Interpretation of tongues—the ability to understand and communicate the words of others who have spoken in tongues, even though the language is unknown. _____

Pastoring (Shepherding)—the ability to guide and care for a group of Christians as they experience spiritual growth. _____

GROUP 6
Miracles—the ability to effectively call on God to do supernatural acts that glorify God. _____

Administration—the ability to organize information, events, or material to work efficiently for the body of Christ. _____

Apostleship—the ability to see the overall picture and respond by starting new churches, pioneering new ministries that impact multiple churches, or ministering transculturally. _____

Evangelism—the desire and ability to share the gospel with those who don't know God in a way that provokes them to believe in God. _____

Your uniqueness is very important in choosing where and how you will serve as a Christian in the church and community. There are no right or wrong gifts. We need a variety of gifts operating through a variety of people to balance the church and have all areas functioning well.

Fruit and Gifts

The difference between spiritual fruit and a spiritual gift is an important concept to understand. Let's look at those differences more closely.

Fruit of the Spirit . . .

All nine character qualities:
- Are present in every believer and are to be developed
- Deal with character—determine who you are
- Develop progressively over time through a lifelong journey
- Are the goal for every Christian
- Define what a Christian is

Gifts of the Spirit . . .
- Are different for every Christian—every believer has a grouping of gifts but not the whole list
- Deal with ministry and serving
- Are given at conversion
- Are the means to reach God's goal for the church
- Determine what a Christian does

The Holy Spirit gave us spiritual gifts to equip and build up the body of Christ. Although God gives us spiritual gifts, the gifts God gives are not for us. They are for the church. They are essentially tools God gives so we can build up and serve others. In addition, it is important to keep in mind that spiritual gifts are not marks of maturity in Christ. Having a spiritual gift doesn't mean we have "arrived" spiritually. Far from it! Rather, maturity is measured by how well we express the fruit of the Spirit in our lives and the humility we demonstrate as we use our gifts.

Discovering Your Spiritual Gifts

It is important not only to understand what the gifts are, but also which specific gifts God has given you. Identifying your own spiritual gifts can help you find your place of service within the body of Christ.

There are four ways you can identify or confirm which gifts God has given you:

1. **Listen to your own heart.** God often reveals God's will through our inner desires and passions. We will have excitement, joy, and anticipation for serving in our gifted area. Remember 1 Corinthians 12 tells us that spiritual gifts can be expressed in different ways, according to our passion and internal wiring. For example, the gift of teaching could be equally effective with adults, children, or youth through speaking, writing, or media. You will feel energized and fulfilled when functioning in the area intended for you.

2. **Listen to those followers of Jesus who are closest to you.** Often, God will confirm your suspicions about which gifts you have through the observations and opinions of mature Christians God has placed in your life. This underlines the importance of being a part of an authentic, committed community of believers. In this environment, we can be honest with each other and be supported in the use of our gifts.

3. **Try out the gift.** God will either confirm your gift or steer you in another direction. This week, come up with one way you can test one of your spiritual gifts. For example, if you think you have the gift of exhortation, you could write and send several encouraging cards and letters. Examine the impact of your efforts. Since spiritual gifts are designed to benefit others, you should see positive results as you use your gifts. If you see no results when you experiment with a particular gift, you probably don't have that gift. But that's okay, because there is more than one gift to explore.

4. **The key to identifying and using your spiritual gifts is prayer and more prayer.** The Lord will lead you to accurate discoveries of your gifts if you allow him to guide and direct all your endeavors.

Reflection

Which spiritual gifts did you identify as yours from the spiritual gifts assessment that you completed in Session Six?

_____

_____

_____

What are some of the areas in which you sense a personal interest in using these gifts (with children, youth, adults, in education, through missions, etc.)?

_____

_____

_____

How can you test your spiritual gifts by serving others this week?

_____

_____

_____

Prayer

I thank you, God, for the ways that you are preparing me to serve other people in God's name, and for empowering me to serve others effectively. Guide me in confirming my gifts and using them in ways that will best serve the church.

Homework

Read and complete Session Eight, including writing down your spiritual journey using the outline provided. Be prepared to share your personal testimony with one or more persons in the class next week. For maximum effectiveness, plan your testimony to be shared within three or four minutes, with most emphasis placed on the difference knowing Jesus has made in your life.

8

SESSION EIGHT
SHARING THE SPIRIT

An important part of being a Christian is sharing your spiritual journey with others as a means of pointing others to a relationship with Jesus or encouraging them in their own walk with Christ. For some of the group this may be a very short journey because you are new in your walk with Christ. For others, the journey will cover a longer period of time. Even people who are still considering whether or not to become a Christian have a story to tell.

The apostle Paul often shared his spiritual journey with others to encourage them to follow God's call in their own lives. As Christians venture out and share how God is working in their lives, they encourage others who might be hesitant or afraid of turning over their life to Christ.

As you share your spiritual journey with others, remember to stay focused on how learning about Jesus or becoming a

Christian is transforming your life. Talk about the impact Christ has had on your life.

Sharing Your Story

When you share your spiritual journey with others, it is always helpful to organize your thoughts by writing out what you want to say. Aim to share enough information to fill three to four minutes. Begin by following these steps:

1. Share about your life before you became a Christian (or before you learned about who Jesus is). You do not need to give intimate details, but focus on the events or feelings that have compelled you to search for the truth.

_____

_____

_____

_____

2. Write how you came to a faith relationship with Christ. At what point did you realize that Jesus was the primary focus of your life?

_____

_____

_____

_____

3. Describe how God has changed you and what God is doing in your life today. If you are not yet a Christian, share how learning about Christ has impacted you personally and the roadblocks you think may be keeping you from deciding to become a Christian now.

_____

_____

_____

_____

The Last Supper

Regularly participating in the experience of Holy Communion is an ongoing reminder of the reality and intimacy of our connection with Jesus.

Read Luke 22:7-20.

Jesus and his disciples met for what would be Jesus' last celebration of Passover or, as it is now called, the Last Supper. At this meal, Jesus shared unleavened bread with his disciples. Traditionally, the unleavened bread was a reminder of Israel's hurried departure from Egypt centuries before, as God miraculously released them from slavery in Egypt. However, during the Last Supper the bread became more. In Luke 22:19, Jesus said, "This is my body given for you; do this in remembrance of me." He also shared a cup of wine with the disciples, and said, "This cup is the new covenant in my blood, which is poured out for you" (Luke 22:20, NIV).

Communion is the most intimate act of the human life—it is where we acknowledge and celebrate our connection with God through Jesus. While sharing bread and wine are symbolic, in some way Jesus actually meets us in the elements.

So, Communion is not to be entered into lightly. It is not something you "just do," or it becomes simply a ritual. In 1 Corinthians 11, Paul counsels believers to approach Communion with great respect and gratitude. Careful self-evaluation must be done ahead of the taking of the elements, confessing any revealed areas of sin that are separating us from God. Since it is the

> Holy Communion is a sacrament, an act of worship, ordained by Christ and is to be observed on a regular basis. All Christians are welcome at our table, whatever their denomination. Communion reminds us of God's great gift of love: God's Son, given for us and all people, his body broken in our place, and his blood shed on our behalf. Three essential messages are clear in the Communion service we celebrate: "Christ has died; Christ is risen; Christ will come again."

reminder of the death and resurrection of Jesus and the awesome sacrifice made on our behalf, we must always approach this earnestly and honestly, not taking it for granted.

When we share in this meal, we proclaim that we are followers of Jesus. We declare our willingness to join him in spreading love throughout the world, even if it means that we may suffer for it sometimes. We are one with Jesus and his mission. If Jesus unites us, then naturally we must be one with one another. We are all fed from the same loaf and drink from the same cup of God's love. This love unites us with God and with each other, so the meal is called Communion, meaning "united with."

Read Luke 24:28-34.

In Luke's Resurrection story, the risen Christ broke bread with two of his followers at Emmaus, "then their eyes were opened, and they recognized him" (24:31, NIV). So, as we are nourished by this meal, our eyes are opened; and we recognize Christ in our lives, in our congregation, in our community, and in our world. Our response is thanksgiving—or in Greek, *Eucharisteas*, "gave thanks."

Reflection

The breaking of the unleavened bread was a Jewish ritual. What do you learn about the Passover in Exodus 12:3-28?

_____

_____

_____

What does Jeremiah say about the new covenant in Jeremiah 31:31 that sets it apart from the covenant found in the Old Testament? Read Jeremiah 31:31-34.

_____

_____

_____

Prayer

I praise you, God, for each person in my study group (name them individually now). Thank you for each person's presence and impact in the group. Thank you for what you are doing in them and through them. I claim your promise to be with each of us as we seek to share our spiritual journey with others this week.

Homework

Share your spiritual journey with someone this week. Read and complete Session Nine.

Part 3
Living in Faith and Service

9

SESSION NINE
SPIRITUAL DISCIPLINES:
KEYS TO GOD'S HEART

Have you ever lost your keys? We don't often think much about keys, but they are clearly important for us to have in order to get where we need to go and do what we need to do each day. The same principle is true in our spiritual lives. Through the Bible, God teaches us about specific "keys" (spiritual disciplines) that we need to have and use in order to get where we need to go spiritually. These are keys to God's heart that open up an intimate relationship with our Creator.

Defining Spiritual Disciplines

The keys to God's heart are what we use to seek God. These keys are called spiritual disciplines because they are life practices that come by choice in our lives. These disciplines are a means to an end—intimacy with Jesus, as we live in the fruit of the Holy Spirit and fulfill God's purpose for us. To reach this intimacy, we have these tools or life practices at our disposal; but we must harness our internal discipline to use them.

Webster's *New World Dictionary* defines discipline as "training that develops self-control" (Second College Edition [Simon and Schuster, 1982]; p. 401). Internal discipline is the ability to choose God's way. It involves a series of choices we make over and over to allow God to control our nature and develop us into our best selves, becoming like Jesus. Using these disciplines is something we decide to do and work at; it doesn't happen automatically. Spiritual disciplines are not generally what we do naturally or easily; but once we choose to incorporate them into our lives on a regular and consistent basis, they become rewarding habits that produce positive results in our lives.

Read Hebrews 12:10-11.
According to these verses, what positive results will you experience in your life as a result of discipline? _____

_____

Why do you think God didn't make spiritual growth automatic?

_____

As an adult, are you now glad that your parents did or did not discipline you? Why or why not? _____

_____

What does your response say about the value of discipline in personal or spiritual growth? _____

_____

A parent disciplines a child to help the child learn and to keep the child safe from harm. God's children are disciplined so they may share in God's holiness. God's discipline produces a harvest of righteousness and peace for those who have been trained by it.

Spiritual disciplines have been compared to the process a farmer goes through when he plants a crop. He cultivates the land, plants the seeds, and then continues to care for the seeds—watering, hoeing, and so forth—until they mature for harvest. The process of cultivating, planting, and caring for the seeds allowed the seeds to grow into what they were meant to become.

As Christians practice spiritual disciplines, we allow the Holy Spirit to work in us so that we may grow into what God meant for us to become.

As we keep using these tools, we allow the Holy Spirit to change and refine us into Christ's image and we will become the person God had in mind even before we were born. Using the spiritual disciplines is much more than going through an activity as part of a daily "to do" list. The disciplines are not an end in themselves or a way to earn favor with God. They are tools that help us seek God, get to know Jesus better and to live life as he taught. We will grow in relationship with our Creator and experience the peace that only connection with that Creator can bring.

The classic spiritual disciplines include:

Bible study
Prayer
Meditation
Worship
Simplicity
Giving
Fasting
Witnessing
Journaling
Solitude
Submission
Service
Confession
Guidance

Read Jeremiah 29:13.

"When you search for me, you will find me;
if you seek me with all your heart."

What do you think it means to seek God with all your heart?

_____

_____

Have you ever wanted something "with all your heart"? What was that like? Can you imagine seeking God with that intensity?

_____

_____

We will find God if we seek God wholeheartedly. We may passionately want to know God personally; but we need a focus for that passion, a way to direct it, hone it, and point it toward God's heart. The spiritual disciplines give us the focus and direction our passion needs to help us know God. Followers of Jesus have used them as instruments for personal spiritual growth for thousands of years. As we discipline ourselves to consistently use these tools, we open ourselves to the Holy Spirit to change and refine us.

One discipline that challenges many is that of giving—but as we understand God's stand on generosity from the Bible, its practice is understandably important for the new believer and for the community.

Included in this lesson is information on biblical generosity, which develops as a result of the spiritual discipline of giving. Read "Biblical Lifestyle of Generosity" (pages 83–84) and answer the following questions:

- What speaks to you from this statement on giving? _____

  _____

  _____

- What do you believe are the biggest challenges to giving in line with biblical standards, and what are the best ways to overcome those challenges? _____

  _____

Reflection

Which spiritual disciplines are you currently practicing on a consistent basis? _____

_____

_____

Which other spiritual discipline do you believe God wants to use to transform your life? _____

_____

_____

How will you start implementing this discipline into your time with God this week? _____

_____

_____

Prayer

Thank you, God, for giving us spiritual disciplines that draw us into your presence and help us build intimacy with you every day. Help me strengthen my resolve to practice these disciplines and to trust that you will meet with me as I do.

Homework

Read and complete Session Ten.

Biblical Lifestyle of Generosity

Throughout the Scriptures, God emphasizes that people who follow God are to also reflect the nature of God. An overpowering characteristic of God is generosity. We are taught to give as God gives to us. As the Holy Spirit lives in us, our lives reflect God's lifestyle of generosity.

In the Old Testament, God, the Creator and Owner of everything, was very clear in expecting us to reciprocate in the giving process. As God freely gives to us, that same attitude is expected in return.

A term introduced in the Old Testament is *tithe*. The Law required the giving of tithes, or one-tenth of a person's gross income, to God. This was seen as a mandatory gift that supported the leaders and activities of God's ministry. The people were assured that in spite of required giving, God would meet their daily needs.

As the story unfolds, three responses to God's mandate to give emerged. Some of God's people became casualties of a common struggle—greed. In order to have more for themselves, they stopped giving their ten percent. The second response involved people who continued to give, but out of duty and obligation, not out of love for God. Thirdly, there was always the faithful core who continued in giving as God directed.

As we move into the New Testament, we sense a shift in the emphasis on the amount to give. New covenant believers, recognizing that they are under the Lordship (ownership) of God, see all of their income as belonging to God—not just the tithe. In fact, the New Testament model is that Christians are to keep only what they need to provide for themselves and their families. While freely giving, they are not to become a drain on the resources of others. So we must ask ourselves, "What is a reasonable amount required to meet my family's current and future needs?" The amount beyond this is what is given to promote God's work.

The New Testament takes the Old Testament standard to a new level: generosity. This explains the minimal amount of direct teaching in the New Testament on the subject of tithing. According to the New Testament, tithing is only the beginning of giving. For Christians whose income is limited and barely meets their needs, tithing is a goal to achieve. For wealthier Christians, whose income exceeds their needs, the tithe becomes restrictive. We are to go beyond tithing in proportion to how God gives to us. We are to be channels for the resources of God to flow through, not dams holding back God's goodness for ourselves.

It is appropriate for a local church to expect their members to contribute at least a tenth of their income to that local church. This enables the local church to operate as God intended, and both Old and New Testaments support such a stand. Beyond the tithe, giving becomes gifts and offering to God's work.

10

SESSION TEN
THE CHURCH: COMMUNITY OF CHRIST

In Session Nine we talked about the growth and transformation that is stimulated by the consistent practice of spiritual disciplines. In this lesson we will talk about the growth and transformation that happens through active participation in the community of Christ—the church. Today's session will be a time of thinking and learning about the church and its role and purpose.

The Church

Read the following excerpt from the book *In His Image* by Dr. Paul Brand and Philip Yancey:

Jesus, the exact likeness of God in flesh, expressed the image of God in human form. But from the very beginning He warned that His physical presence was temporary. He had in mind a further goal: to restore the broken image of God in humanity.

God's activity on earth did not end with Jesus, and His image on earth did not vanish when Jesus departed. New Testament authors extend the term to a new Body God is creating composed of "members"—men and women joining together to do the work of God. In referring to this Body, these writers pointedly used the same word that first described the spark of the divine in man and later described Christ. We are called, said Paul, to be "the likeness [image] of his Son, that he might be the firstborn among many brothers" (Romans 8:29b). (Zondervan, 1984; pages 39–40)

How is the description of the church in this excerpt similar or different from your perception or experience of the church?

_____

_____

_____

The church consists of men and women joining together to do the work of God. When Jesus left the earth, he left his mission in his followers' hands. We are God's representatives on earth, called to help restore the broken image of God in humanity. Our mission is to seek those lost to God and to set those who are physically, spiritually, emotionally, and relationally oppressed free in Christ. God chooses to work through us to accomplish God's purpose in the lives of others.

The church is more than an organization or structure. It is an organism that is made up of living parts—a living representation of Christ on earth. It is not a perfect representation by any means because it is filled with imperfect people like you and me. In 2 Corinthians 4:6-7, the apostle Paul described humans as "jars of clay"—frail and fallible human beings. It is through just such "broken vessels" that God chooses to be revealed to the world. It is through such "broken vessels" that God releases the power to bring about God's desired outcome for the world.

What Is the Church?

In the Bible God uses the metaphor of the body to help us understand the interconnectedness of Christ's followers on earth. Just like the human body, the spiritual body of Christ is made up of living, breathing parts, all controlled by the head. Each follower of Jesus is a part of the body, intimately connected to and needed by the other parts. Each of us receives instructions from the head (Jesus), lives under Jesus' authority and control, and passes those instructions on to the parts of the body connected to us.

Read through the following Scriptures about what the church is. Make notes in the spaces provided about the terms used to describe the church and any other insights you have.

• Acts 2:44-47 _____

• Romans 12:4-5 _____

• 1 Corinthians 12:12-14, 27 _____

• 1 Corinthians 12:21-25 _____

• 2 Corinthians 6:18 _____

• Ephesians 2:19-20 _____

• Ephesians 4:3-6 _____

• Revelation 19:6-8 _____

• Revelation 21:1-3 _____

What do you see in these verses that describes the identity and characteristics of the church?

_____
_____
_____

How do these descriptions compare with what you have experienced with the church?

_____

_____

_____

It is interesting to note the terms used in Scripture to describe the connection between God and God's followers, and the connection between individual followers of Jesus. The Bible uses words like *body*, *bride*, *family*, and *community*. Each of those terms describes a group of people bound together by commitment, deep care, and common interests, beliefs, and values. Marriage, family, and community are covenantal relationships, meaning they are relationships based on covenants, vows, and promises. Participants in those relationships are called to long-term commitment, living together for better or worse by demonstrating the faithfulness of God to each other. Obviously God takes the connection with God and with other followers seriously.

Scripture also consistently uses the term *unity* to describe these relationships. While each of us is created to be unique and to have a unique place within the body, God expects harmony among us. In other words, God wants a unified body but doesn't require uniformity. We celebrate individual differences and the joy of diversity. There may be areas in which we agree to disagree, but we need to be united on the basic tenets of the faith.

What Is the Purpose of the Church?

The following Scriptures explain why the church is here. Read through these passages to understand more about the purpose of the church on earth. Make notes in the spaces provided concerning the purpose of the church identified in each Scripture passage.

- John 13:34-35 _____
- 1 Corinthians 10:31 _____
- 2 Corinthians 4:5 _____
- Galatians 6:9-10 _____
- Ephesians 2:10 _____
- Ephesians 3:20-21 _____
- Ephesians 4:11-12 _____
- 2 Timothy 4:1-2 _____
- Hebrews 10:24-25 _____

How would you summarize the purpose of the church?

_____
_____
_____

Since Jesus is no longer here in human form, we are the only hands and feet he has on earth. We are God's distribution system. We are to continue Jesus' mission, in the power of the Spirit, by demonstrating love, spreading his word, serving, equipping the saints for ministry, and above all, glorifying and honoring God. Together, through our combined gifts, we touch the world for Jesus.

In order for the church to fulfill its role in the world, we must each personally discover and fulfill our roles in the church, both locally and globally. Every church, though organic in nature, needs to be organized to help each person find his or her place to serve within the body of Christ.

If you have questions about how your church is organized or about the membership expectations, ask your study leader or pastor.

Conclusion

The church is not a building where people go but God's people in community doing what God has called us to do. The church is a living organism that brings change to the people of the world. We know Christ through worship, study, prayer, submission, and obedience. We make Christ known to others through loving, teaching, serving, and sharing our faith.

There is a place reserved for you within this organism called the body of Christ, including a specific purpose to serve for the benefit of others. It is important that we each discover God's unique call on our lives. In Session Eleven we will investigate how to go about discovering God's call for each of us.

Reflection

Take a few minutes to prayerfully assess what God's call might be for you within the body of Christ. Where do you think God might want you to serve others within Christ's body?

Prayer

I praise you, God, for allowing me to be a part of the body and mission of God here on earth. Thank you for the church family where we each find inspiration and support for our part of God's mission. Guide me in how and where you want me to serve.

Homework

If you are considering committing to membership at your local church, please ask your study leader for a membership interview form, complete it, and bring it to your one-on-one conference with one of your church leaders. This form is simply a preparation for your time with a church leader before membership weekend. It is an affirmation of who you are and your commitment to the church. It is also a place to indicate where you feel called to serve within the church body and be helped in making that connection. Check with your leader about how to sign up for your interview. Read and complete Session Eleven.

11

SESSION ELEVEN
UNDERSTANDING
GOD'S CALL

As a follower of Christ, you are experiencing life's great unfolding adventure—discovering God's call on your life. Although many of us say that we chose Jesus, the reality is that Jesus first chose us (John 15:16). Jesus chose us to be about his business, which is reaching out to those who do not yet know him and joining with others to serve in Jesus' name.

Sometimes we may think that the pastor and church staff—the "paid professionals"—are the ones called by God to do God's work. A look at the New Testament church of the first century gives insight into how God's church is to operate.

Read Acts 8:1-4.

• How was the church dispersed from Jerusalem to Judea and Samaria? What did those scattered do? _____

_____

• What is the significance of ordinary people being given responsibility for fulfilling God's mission on earth? _____

_____

• What are different ways that the Word can be "preached"? Which way do you feel God has equipped you to share the good news about Jesus? _____

_____

As the result of persecution, the early church spread throughout the known world. There was not an expectation of the apostles doing all the work. In fact, it was the ordinary people, who had been forced out of Jerusalem, who were preaching the Word wherever they went. There was no longer a separation between the priesthood and ordinary followers as there had been in the Old Testament system. The understanding in the new covenant is that all Christ's followers function as priests: representing people to God and representing God to people. Each follower has been given a custom-designed way of doing that by God.

To discover God's call on our lives, we have to take time to look inward and ask ourselves some meaningful questions about our passions and our desires, as well as our gifts and abilities. In this session, you will go on a private, inward journey.

Discovering God's Call

Read Psalm 139:13-16.

There is a plan for each one of us that is specifically designed by God and prepared for us before time began. This is what we refer to as our call from God. Each of us in our Christian walk must answer the questions: *What is my call?* and *How do I personally carry out the ministry of Jesus?*

To proceed with this quest, it helps to follow a plan that leads us in discovering what God has created us to do. This plan is repeatable; you can go through the steps of this plan each time you are trying to discern the next step in God's call for you.

The first step in discovering God's call on your life is to surrender yourself to God.

Read Matthew 16:24-25 and Romans 12:1-2.

We must surrender everything to Jesus. Surrender is not easy for any of us. We are taught to be independent, self-sufficient, make-your-own-decision kind of people. But to allow Jesus to be Lord, we must surrender ourselves to him and give him permission to carry out his plan through us.

Are there areas of your life that you sense need to be surrendered to God? Write those here: _____

_____

Now, take a few moments to silently give those areas to God. As you do so, thank God for God's forgiveness and willingness to be Lord of your life.

The second step is to listen to God.

Read Jeremiah 29:11-13 and Deuteronomy 30:19-20.

Through the Word of God, we learn that our Creator has a plan for each of us. God will tell us what that plan is and guide us step by step if we take time to listen. Even though we know God is loving and just, we may be fearful of what we will hear or what God may ask us to do. This fear is unnecessary because God's will for our lives is born out of God's love for us. We must be willing to risk, lay aside our reservations, and listen to God. Only by listening can we discern God's call for our lives.

Take some time now and listen to God in silence. As you listen, write down anything you think the Holy Spirit is saying to you. Be sensitive to the thoughts and internal nudges that may be God speaking to you. Throughout life, you will hear God in many ways—through God's Word, through silent prayer like you are practicing now, or through the voices of other people speaking to you. The assurance is that over time you will learn to recognize God's voice and train yourself to respond in obedience.

_____

_____

_____

The third step is to confirm who is speaking.

Once you believe you have heard from God, the next step is to test what you have heard. Not everything we think we hear really comes from God. There are many other voices within us competing for attention. Our own desires, fears, and the voice of the enemy all battle for dominance in our attempts to hear God in our spirits.

Below are some of the questions you must ask yourself to determine whether the call you hear is really from God or from some other source. If you cannot answer yes to all these questions, then you may need to rethink whether the call you have heard is really from God.

Is it scriptural? Is the call you are considering consistent with the commands and principles of God's Word? God will never call you to do anything that goes against what is taught in Scripture. _____

_____

Does it glorify Christ? The purpose of following God's call is not to glorify or call attention to us, but to point others to Jesus and life in him. Anything that glorifies a person above God or dishonors Christ is not of God. _____

Is it my passion? God created each of us to be unique. Each of us has different things that bring us joy. God's plan for us is designed to fit the way we are made. As a result, we often have a strong desire to serve in a way that fits with the deepest desires of our hearts. ___

___

Is it consistent with my gifts and talents? If we are searching for the way God will use us, it only makes sense that God's plan for us would match up with and use the spiritual gifts and talents God has given us. What talents and gifts has God given you? Do these match up with the call you are considering? _____

___

Does it meet a need? As you look around the community where you live, can you see how this call can genuinely help other people? God does not call us to do things that are purely self-focused. Anything God calls us to do has the ultimate goal of serving others, meeting their needs, and helping them to know God. _____

___

What is the counsel of other believers? Those believers who know you well can give you wise counsel as you attempt to discover God's will for you. Being a part of a small group where you are prayer for, encouraged, and held accountable will develop friends who can give you honest feedback and share with you what you may not be able to see for yourself. _____

Take a few moments to assess what you believe God may be saying to you about God's call for you. Answer each of the above questions on the lines provided with that in mind.

The fourth step is trusting God.

Following God can seem risky because we give up control over our own destinies. Where will God take us? What will God call us to do? Will God protect us and keep us from making mistakes? *Read Deuteronomy 7:9; 1 Corinthians 1:4-9; and Psalm 22:5.*

God is not safe in the human sense of the word. The Bible makes it clear that God can and will allow God's children to make mistakes and to suffer. But God is good and intends the best possible outcome for us. And that is why we can trust God, wherever God leads. When we step out in faith, God will not disappoint us. We can depend on God to be faithful in keeping God's promises.

Reflection

Take the next moments to prayerfully answer the following questions:

What did you learn about yourself during your study of this session?

_____

_____

_____

What did you learn about discovering God's call on your life?

_____

_____

_____

What's one way you think God has called you to serve?

_____

_____

_____

We have talked about unique, personal calls from God on the lives of God's followers. But there are some things all Christians are called to do, such as loving one another, supporting God's mission with our tithes and gifts, sharing our faith, and pursuing a Christ-like lifestyle. Even as you are exploring a specific call God has placed on your life, you can serve God by obediently doing those things.

Prayer

Write a brief prayer to God. Tell God how you feel about the call God has placed on your life and how you feel about letting go of your own plans in favor of God's plans for you. Ask God to strengthen your faith so that you can follow God's will boldly, with all your heart. Thank God for choosing you and for the unique call God has placed on your life. Let God know that you trust God to reveal your call to you a step at a time.

Homework

Read and complete Session Twelve.

12

SESSION TWELVE
GOD'S PLACE FOR YOU

Can you think of a time recently when you used an excuse to avoid doing something? We all use silly excuses at times to get out of doing things. Sometimes we even use excuses to avoid things we really want to do but are afraid to try. We may be afraid of failure (or success), or perhaps we're afraid we will make the wrong choice. That's how it often is for Christians when they first step out to serve in the church. Deep down they may really want to serve; but they are afraid, so they make excuses.

If that has been your experience, don't worry. You are in good company! Even Moses, one of the greatest followers of God in the Bible, made excuses when God called him at the burning bush. Let's look at some of the excuses Moses made. I suspect that at least some of them will look familiar.

Read Exodus 3:1-10.

• Describe how and to what God is calling Moses.

_____

_____

_____

• In what ways have you heard God's call?

_____

_____

_____

For each of the following Scripture readings, identify the excuse Moses made to God to justify not fulfilling God's call on his life. Then answer the questions below.

"But Moses said to God, "Who am I that I should go to Pharaoh and bring the Israelites out of Egypt?" (Exodus 3:11)

• Exodus 3:11-12 _____

_____

• Exodus 3:13-15 _____

_____

• Exodus 4:1-9 _____

_____

• Exodus 4:10-12 _____

_____

• Exodus 4:13-17 _____

_____

Are any of these excuses familiar? _____
What are modern-day equivalent excuses that Christians use? ____

_____

How can you, like Moses, overcome your excuses in order for God to use you? _____

100

Using Your Call

In Session Eleven, we walked through the steps involved in discovering the call God has placed upon each one of us. Today we'll go one step further to come to an understanding of where to use that call within the church and our local community by looking at how your passions and gifts work together. To do that, follow the directions in these three areas:

Your Passions

To discover your passions, write down your answers to the following questions:

If you had no restrictions on your time or money, what kinds of people or special causes would you like to help?

_____

_____

_____

What group of people or special cause would you like to serve in order to leave a legacy or make a difference?

_____

_____

_____

What would your spouse or closest friend say you are passionate about?

_____

_____

_____

Your Spiritual Gifts

Think about the spiritual gifts God has given you. Go back and review Session Seven about spiritual gifts. Write down your spiritual gifts that you identified from that session.

_____

_____

_____

Your Personality Style

To help identify your personality style, or how God has wired you, write down your answers to the following questions:

Do you prefer to work with people or do you prefer to work on a task without interacting with people very much?

_____

_____

_____

Do you prefer doing things that require you to lead, plan, and organize events or people or do you prefer to work in a supporting role behind the scenes?

_____

_____

_____

Now, to find your place in the local church and community, pull the information from these three areas together. Is there a kind of service in which all of these areas intersect? Think about ways of serving your church and community that will use your passions, spiritual gifts, and personality style. Write down your ideas and discuss them with your study leader or small group leader.

Reflection

Everything we have studied in the last twelve sessions can be summed up in the word *discipleship*. We have discovered God's expectations of God's children. It is now up to you to take this information and let it, in the power of the Holy Spirit, transform your life.

Prayer

Lord, thank you for your presence and your movement in my life through this study. I praise you for daily opportunities to be transformed into Christ's image. I pray for the leaders and other participants in this study as they too take the next step in discipleship and service to God. Thank you for their influence on my spiritual growth.

Homework

Work with your church leaders to find a place of service and a small group of other believers for accountability and encouragement. Then serve and live passionately and wholeheartedly.

Evaluation

We are so glad that you have been part of this study. Your presence has helped encourage all of us! We celebrate how far we've come together. It would be helpful to us to hear your thoughts on your experience in this class. Please answer these last three questions:

1. What has been especially meaningful to you in the past twelve sessions?

_____

_____

_____

2. Which sessions have you taken to heart and already implemented in your life?

_____

_____

_____

3. What is the next step in your discipleship process?

_____

_____

_____

When you are finished, please leave your answers with your study leader.